Pioneer Girl

Pioneer Girl

GROWING UP ON THE PRAIRIE

Andrea Warren

SCHOLASTIC INC.

New York Toronto London Auckland Sydney
Mexico City New Delhi Hong Kong

For my parents, Ruth & J. V. Warren,
and for Ben, always

ISBN 0-439-18820-2

12 11 10 9 8 7 6 5 4 3 2 1   0 1 2 3 4 5/0

Printed in the U.S.A.   23

First Scholastic printing, March 2000

DESIGNED BY RACHEL SIMON

RIGHT: Grace McCance as a baby, before her family moved to Nebraska

A NOTE TO READERS

*T*his true story of Grace McCance Snyder is based on interviews with her family and on the memories of her childhood recorded in her memoir, *No Time on My Hands,* written by her daughter, Nellie Snyder Yost. Many other sources were also used in preparing this book.

Grace had a remarkable memory and could recall details from even her very early years. Whenever she is quoted, the words are directly from her memoir. The families of Grace McCance Snyder and Nellie Snyder Yost have given generous permission for the use of information and quotations from *No Time on My Hands* (Lincoln: University of Nebraska Press, 1986. Copyright 1963 by Nellie Snyder Yost. Epilogue copyright 1986 by the University of Nebraska Press).

Contents

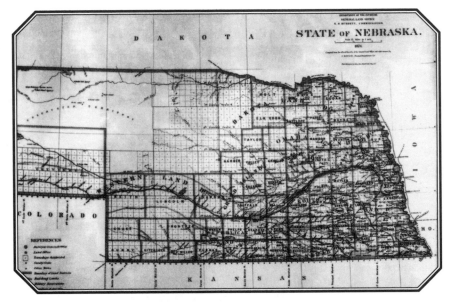

Nebraska in the 1880s

INTRODUCTION

When I was growing up in Newman Grove, Nebraska, I could see a cornfield from my bedroom window, and I marked the seasons by its growth and colors. My view now is of city streets, and I sometimes wish I could still see that cornfield every day as a reminder of the pioneer families who settled the Midwest.

Many pioneer children grew up on hardscrabble homesteads, working alongside their parents in harsh conditions to nurture the growth of crops and cattle. In researching the lives of children on the prairie, however, I did not hear many complaints. These children were needed by their families and had a strong sense of purpose. Because they knew no other life, they did not feel deprived. The prairie was their home. Their optimism, steadfastness, and hard work have given those of us fortunate enough to live in this beautiful part of the world a proud legacy.

When I first read Grace McCance Snyder's memoir, *No Time on My Hands,* I knew I wanted to write about her pioneer childhood. I liked her spunk and spirit. She dared to dream, and she saw her dreams come true.

I hope readers will enjoy her story as it is told here and, through her, will gain a new appreciation of what it meant to grow up on the prairie.

—A.W.

RICH FARMING LANDS!

ON THE LINE OF THE

Union Pacific Railroad!

Located in the **GREAT CENTRAL BELT** of **POPU-LATION, COMMERCE** and **WEALTH,** and adjoining the **WORLD'S HIGHWAY** from **OCEAN TO OCEAN.**

12,000,000 ACRES!

3,000,000 Acres in Central and Eastern Nebraska, in the Platte Valley, now for sale!

We invite the attention of all parties seeking a HOME, to the LANDS offered for sale by this Company.

The Vast Quantity of Land from which to select, enables every one to secure such a location as he desires, suitable to any branch of farming or stock raising.

The Prices are Extremely Low. The amount of land owned by the Company is so large that they are determined to sell at the cheapest possible rates, ranging from $1.50 to $8.00 per acre.

The Terms of Payment are Easy. Ten years' credit at six per cent interest. A deduction of ten per cent for cash.

The Location is Central, along the 41st parallel, the favorite latitude of America. Equally well adapted to corn or wheat; free from the long, cold winters of the Northern, and the hot, unhealthy influences of the Southern States.

The Face of the Country is diversified with hill and dale, grain land and meadow, rich bottoms, low bluffs, and undulating tables, all covered with a thick growth of sweet nutritious grasses.

The Soil is a dark loam, slightly impregnated with lime, free from stone and gravel, and eminently adapted to grass, grain and root crops; the subsoil is usually light and porous, retaining moisture with wonderful tenacity.

The Climate is mild and healthful; the atmosphere dry and pure. Epidemic diseases never prevail; Fever and Ague are unknown. The greatest amount of rain falls between March and October. The Winters are dry with but little snow.

The Productions are wheat, corn, oats, barley, rye and root crops, and vegetables generally. Flax, sweet potatoes, sorghum, etc., etc., do well and yield largely.

Fruits, both Wild and Cultivated, do remarkably well. The freedom from frosts in May and September, in connection with the dry Winters and warm soil, renders this State eminently adapted to fruit culture.

Stock Raising in all its branches, is particularly profitable on the wide ranges of rich pasturage. Cattle and sheep feed with avidity and fatten upon the nutritious grasses without grain; hogs thrive well, and wool growing is exceedingly remunerative.

Timber is found on the streams and grows rapidly.

Coal of excellent quality, exists in vast quantities on the line of the road in Wyoming, and is furnished to settlers at reduced rates.

Market Facilities are the best in the West; the great mining regions of Wyoming, Colorado, Utah and Nevada, are supplied by the farmers of Platte Valley.

The Title given the purchaser is absolute, in fee simple, and free from all incumbrances, derived directly from the United States.

Soldiers of the Late War are entitled to a Homestead of one hundred and sixty acres, within Railroad limits, which is equal to a bounty of $400.

Persons of Foreign Birth are also entitled to the benefits of the Free Homestead Law, on declaring their intentions of becoming citizens of the United States; this they may do immediately on their arrival in this country.

For Colonies, the lands on the line of the Union Pacific Railroad afford the *best locations* in the West.

TOWN LOTS FOR SALE VERY CHEAP in the most important towns on the line of the Road, affording excellent opportunities for business or investments.

Full information in regard to lands, prices, terms of sale, &c., together with pamphlets, circulars and maps, may be obtained from all the Agents of the Department, also the

"PIONEER."

A handsome ILLUSTRATED PAPER, with maps, etc., and containing the HOMESTEAD LAW. *Mailed free* to all applicants. Address

O. F. DAVIS,
Land Commissioner, U. P. R. R.

OMAHA, NEB.

Posters like this one, advertising land for sale by the railroad, drew settlers to the prairie.

A Home in the Promised Land

Grace McCance scrambled down the steps of the train, planted her feet on the muddy ground, and looked around. So *this* was Nebraska! No trees blocked the view, and she liked the bigness of it.

Florry, whose real name was Flora Alice, followed her off the train. Florry was five, two years older than Grace. She stepped cautiously, avoiding mud puddles so she would not get her dress or shoes dirty. Then their mother, Margaret McCance, appeared at the train doorway carrying baby Stella and a heavy travel satchel. She looked tired from the trip. The girls waved at her. She nodded, then lifted her stylish black skirt and slowly descended the steep train steps.

"Poppie!" Grace cried, catching sight of her father driving up in the old wagon pulled by the family mules. She ran to meet him and threw herself into his arms the moment he jumped down. Charles McCance embraced his family. He grinned as he kissed Mama. They had last seen him three months earlier when he loaded the family's belongings into a train boxcar, urged the mules aboard, and then hopped in himself for the long ride to Nebraska.

Folks back home in Missouri said Poppie had "land fever" because he had decided to become a homesteader. The 1862 Homestead Act allowed him to file a claim on 160 acres of public land. If he built a house and cultivated the soil, in five years the land would be his. Men or women who were single or heads of households could file a homestead claim as long as they were twenty-one and were either citizens or immigrants who planned to become citizens. Early in the spring of 1885, Poppie had found his claim near the town of Cozad in central Nebraska. He paid the ten-dollar filing fee and set to work. His first task had been to build a house so he could send for his family—and now they were here.

Everyone settled into the wagon, and Poppie turned the mules toward the northwest. When they stopped several hours later, Grace woke up from a nap. She thought they must be in the middle of nowhere. She recalled in her memoir, "I can still see the homestead as it looked when we pulled into it that day—just two naked little soddies squatting on a bare, windswept ridge. . . . Not another building in sight, not a tree, not an animal, nothing but grassy flats and hills."

The "soddies" were built of blocks of compacted sod Poppie had cut from the earth. The smaller one was a stable. The other was a twelve-by-fourteen-foot room: their new home. It was smaller than Grandmother Blaine's parlor in Missouri. Grace stared at the tiny house. The wind whipped around them, its sound a mournful wail. For a moment she felt unsure about this new place.

Then she saw her cat, Old Tom, who had made the trip with Poppie and the mules, and a moment later she and Florry were running through the prairie grass, laughing. Darting ahead of Mama and Poppie, they explored the house, happy to see the cookstove and the familiar belongings from their old house. Later they walked with Mama and Poppie to see the field Poppie was readying for corn planting. Poppie kept saying this was land where anything would grow. Mama was quiet. The only thing she asked about was a school, but

Sod was such a sturdy building material that settlers called it "Nebraska marble." They often used it for the roof as well as the walls of their houses.

Poppie said the girls were still too young for school, and by the time they were old enough, he figured there would be one.

Thinking back on that first day, Grace realized that, for herself and Florry, "it was all new and interesting, but to Mama it must have seemed poor and desolate. She had grown up among the green fields and woods of Missouri, where she lived in a big white house. She liked nice things, good food, pretty clothes, handsome furniture. I know she must have been nearly crushed by the unexpected bigness of the prairie, the endless blue of the sky, our rough, homemade furniture, and the almost total lack of neighbors."

Many settlers *were* crushed by the experience of homesteading.

The plains and prairies of the Midwest, stretching from the Missouri River on the east to the Rocky Mountains on the west, challenged the most hardy of pioneers. It was country where the wind blew constantly, where few trees grew, where it froze in winter and baked in summer, and where water was scarce. As Grace would learn, anyone who settled there eventually got acquainted with drought, grasshoppers, rattlesnakes, stampedes, prairie fires, dust storms, hail, floods, tornadoes, and blizzards.

Even when the government started the great homestead giveaway to attract settlers to the middle part of the country, many folks wondered why anyone would bother. Most pioneers just passed right through the Midwest on their way to the Far West. Those who stayed were often defeated. One farmer scrawled across the cabin door of his deserted claim, "250 miles to the nearest post office, 100 miles to wood, 20 miles to water, 6 inches to hell. Gone to live with wife's folks."

But whatever Mama thought of the homestead, she was there to stay. She knew what the land meant to her husband. Poppie had been poor all his life. His father had died when Poppie was young, and his mother had struggled to raise her big family. This was his chance to have something of his own. Mama could see how hard he had worked to build the house and to start breaking up the tough sod. She would do her part as well.

According to Grace, "Mama was the kind who always did the best she could with what she had." For the one window on each wall, Mama made curtains out of bleached flour sacks on which she embroidered red birds. She arranged the bed, the cradle, the cookstove, and her sewing machine. She made shelves out of boxes and displayed the English teacup that had been part of her grandmother's wedding dishes. Last of all, she hung the gilt-framed marriage certificate over the marble-topped bureau. Grace thought it made the soddy look elegant.

Poppie also helped make the soddy feel like a home. He built Florry and Grace a trundle bed, which slid under their parents' bed during the day. He laid a wooden floor—something most sod houses didn't have. He plastered and whitewashed the walls so the room would feel bright.

When Grace asked Poppie why he did not build them a wood house, he said the lumber would have to come by railroad and would be too expensive. In this part of the country settlers used the one building material that was cheap and plentiful—unplowed prairie. They jokingly called it "Nebraska marble." It had taken Poppie an acre

A rare photograph of the crowded interior of a one-room sod house

of sod and much hard work to construct their soddy, but the thick root system created walls that were strong and long lasting.

Poppie pointed out the advantages of a soddy. Wood houses usually had no insulation, so they were cold in winter and hot in summer. Sod provided natural insulation, so soddies were more comfortable. Soddies offered more protection than wood houses from fire, wind, and tornadoes. Most families kept their soddies as storm shelters or stables, even after they built wood houses. Some liked them so much they continued to live in them even when they could afford wood houses.

Mama did not intend to stay in a soddy. Soddies had advantages, but they also had drawbacks. Dirt sifted down from the ceiling and walls. During heavy rains, water could work down through the roof and run along the floor, soaking everything and turning the floor to mud. Even after the rains ended, the roof could leak for days. Few homesteaders ever got used to wearing boots and carrying umbrellas inside their soddies when the sun was shining outside.

T W O

Settling In

Like other settlers, the McCances soon learned that rain was only one of the problems of living in a sod house. Newly cut sod often housed fleas. Bedbugs came out at night, crawling all over everything and biting anyone trying to sleep. Bedding had to be dragged outside, the bugs picked off, and then, Grace remembered, "every crack and crevice in the walls and furniture gone over with chicken feathers dipped in kerosene."

At least the McCances did not have the experience of one Kansas settler, who awoke one morning to find the floor, ceilings, and walls covered with inch-long worms. She had to cover her hair and the water pail and sweep the worms outside. It was bad enough that the McCances had to put up with flies, mosquitoes, and moths. They were as plentiful inside as outside because the family could not afford window screens and it was too warm in the soddy with the windows closed.

When Mama cooked food on summer days, the soddy became unbearably hot. Usually the family would set the table outside and eat there. The girls thought this was like having a picnic. It was Grace's job to keep the flies "off the table with a fly-chaser made of newspaper fringe sewed to a long stick."

Field mice and snakes burrowed through the ceiling and walls of the soddy, looking for warmth. Mama shuddered when she heard stories about snakes crawling into babies' beds. Settlers told of snakes dropping down from the rafters, sometimes plopping onto the table during dinner. Before getting out of bed, most people first looked under it and *then* put their feet on the floor.

Mama could tolerate everything except the rattlesnakes. Since homesteaders had invaded the snakes' territory, the snakes could not be blamed for being there. At the same time, settlers could not live side by side with poisonous ones. Rattlesnakes, some six feet long, were common. One day when Mama was outside, a baby chick in the nearby grass suddenly started to squawk. It came running toward Mama, who scooped it up. At that moment, she saw the rattler that had bitten it. She yelled for Poppie, who was in the house. He ran out carrying the teakettle full of boiling water and threw it on the snake, scalding it to death. By then the chick was dead. Mama kept thinking it could have been one of the girls who got bit.

Finding enough fuel to burn for cooking and heat was another problem. The early pioneers had gathered buffalo chips—dried patties of dung left by the millions of buffalo that had roamed the plains for a thousand years. They called these "prairie coal." But the buffalo were all but gone. Droughts had destroyed their food supplies; white hunters had slaughtered them. Poppie said that soon they would have cattle to supply cow chips. In the meantime, he chopped up sunflower stalks and corncobs for fuel. The chopping was hard work, and neither stalks nor cobs made fires as hot and long lasting as chips did.

As for water, Poppie told Mama they would have their own well just as soon as they had enough money to pay a well digger. In the meantime, a nearby shallow pond had water in it for part of the year. They could use it for the animals and to wash clothes, but it was not

Pioneers used buffalo or cow chips for fuel because there were few trees on the prairie. The little girl is holding her corn husk doll.

clean enough for drinking or cooking. For that, they had to haul water from the neighbor's well, two miles away.

Grace learned to conserve every drop of water: "We used it sparingly indeed; saving the washday rinse water, the water we washed vegetables in, even the bath water, to pour into the chicken trough. But no matter how careful we were, the water barrels seemed always nearly empty."

Several times a week Poppie loaded the barrels into the wagon to visit the neighbor's well. Grace and Florry would beg to go along, but Mama almost always said no. She had been raised with a strong sense of respectability. "'I'll not have you girls going off the place unless you're decently dressed in shoes and stockings,'" she would say. The problem during those early years of homesteading was that Grace and Florry hardly ever had good shoes and stockings at the same time, so they rarely were allowed to go anywhere.

Still, they were never bored. Before long, they knew their land better than Poppie did. One of their favorite play spots was an old buffalo wallow—a large hollowed-out area of ground shaped like a bowl, where buffaloes had rolled from side to side, kicking up the earth and throwing dust on themselves to keep insects away. The girls were fascinated by the bleached bones, skulls, and horns they found there.

The one thing they wished for was store-bought dolls, but those were too expensive. Instead, Mama showed them how to make corncob dolls, dressing them from her scrap box with tiny pieces of silk, calico, and ribbon. For hair, they searched out the best corn silk from the cornfield. They made hats out of dried sunflower heads and decorated them with brightly colored feathers. In the soft soil of a clay bank, they created miniature homesteads for their dolls, building dugout houses, roads, fences, and ditches.

Every pioneer child made toys. One girl built a doll's house out of buffalo bones. Another made hats out of the leaves of cottonwood trees. Children carved twigs into whistles. Two boys turned wild melon rinds inside out, strapped them onto their feet, and skated around their cabin floor. In areas where there were huge tumbleweeds, children would tie strings to them and pretend they were horses. One said, "Papa was not always happy with our make-believe horses, for he would lead the real horses into the barn and find our tumbleweeds in the stalls tied to the manger."

When adults chose to become homesteaders, their children had no say in the matter, even though the decision meant they would live hard lives. Grace did not mind. She was strong and energetic, and she

Unlike Grace and Florry, some little girls brought along store-bought dolls to the prairie or had parents who could afford to buy them.

rarely complained about anything. She and Florry immediately accepted the prairie as their home. They possessed what such a life required: They had grit.

So did another little girl whose grandmother in the East told her, "If you go to Kansas, you will have to eat grasshopper soup." The little girl thought about that and then replied bravely, "If Daddy can eat grasshopper soup, I can too." She worried about that soup the whole trip west and was greatly relieved to find that her grandmother was wrong: The ground in Kansas was *not* covered with grasshoppers.

THREE

Getting By

During the spring, Poppie worked from first light until dark, planting the corn. Then he turned his attention to other needs. A well and a cow topped that list, but the move to Nebraska had used up their savings. Poppie weighed his options. The corn could get along without him until it was ready to harvest. He told Mama he thought he should spend the summer helping build the railroad.

Mama was willing to do almost anything to have fresh milk and plenty of water, but she did not want to spend the summer alone on the homestead with three small children. She suggested that she and the girls come with him. Poppie said that would be fine.

That June they joined dozens of other families—mostly other homesteaders in need of cash—in a small campground thirty miles south of Cozad, where the Burlington Railroad was under construction. Poppie had put a cover over the wagon, and they slept in it at night. During the day, while Poppie and the mules helped build the tracks, Mama took care of the children, cooked their food over a fire, and socialized with the other women in the camp.

In early August, Poppie said he had earned enough money. It was time to go home. The homestead was in good shape. There had been

*P*lowing the prairie was backbreaking work.

plenty of rain, and the corn Poppie had planted in the spring was tall and strong. Mama's onions, beans, watermelon, and sweet corn were big and healthy.

The first time Poppie went to town, he stopped by the well company and asked them to come as soon as possible. In the meantime, he continued to fill the water barrels at the neighbor's well. One day he took along some money. He returned with several hens, a rooster, and a little milk cow named Pearlie.

In the fall, Poppie harvested a good corn crop. He gathered hay to feed the livestock over the winter and broke more land for planting in the spring. Then he wrote a letter to his family. He told them that Cozad was growing fast and that he had already grown more beans than he and his relatives had ever raised back home. He also said the men still had not come to dig the well.

They had to wait for the well, but Mama said they could not wait any longer for a cellar, so Poppie dug a cellar cave close to the house. When the tiny underground room was finished, he covered the steps with a wooden door. Cellars provided shelter from bad storms and prairie fires. They were cool and dark, so they were a good place to keep fresh foods like milk and butter and to store canned goods—fruit and vegetables preserved at home in glass jars. Grace loved seeing the rows of "red and green and yellow jars of tomatoes, snap beans, and corn shining like jewels in the dim light in the cave."

Mama had one more project for Poppie. She wanted another room on the soddy before winter came. It was too hard to sleep, cook, and live in one room. Not only did Poppie add on a big room, but he also put in a window with a wide bench seat. Mama loved it. She made a bright carpet of woven rags, and they moved the beds and sewing machine into the room.

Poppie came home from town one day with a high-backed rocking chair for Mama. She placed it by the window and sat in it during the evening while she did her sewing. Sometimes, if she was not too tired, she would sing to Grace, Florry, and the baby or tell them stories. Their favorite stories were about her life as a little girl when she lived in the big white house with a flower garden. She told them how the house had screens on the windows to keep out the flies and how servants helped with the work. Young as she was, Grace sensed that these stories both comforted and troubled her mother. More than anything, Mama wanted a house with a proper front parlor where nobody had to sleep.

But right now a small house was better so they could keep it warm in winter when fuel was scarce. They needed their house to protect them from bad weather and give them a place to sleep and prepare food and make soap and candles. Anything decorative, including family treasures like clocks, photo albums, and good china, had to be squeezed in among necessary everyday items.

Mama worked as hard as Poppie. Her most important daily chore was food preparation. The three children ate a lot. So did their father. Grace and Florry helped gather eggs and hunt for wild berries, nuts, and herbs. Mama made jams and jellies from the berries, or dried them. She used fresh or preserved vegetables and potatoes from the garden. She cut sweet corn off the cobs and dried it in the sun, turning it frequently until it was crisp and brown, so it could be combined with boiling water and eaten as hot cereal in the winter. She baked bread and biscuits. As soon as she had milk, eggs, and butter to cook with, she made muffins, cakes, custards, and pies. For meat they had rabbits, quail, and prairie chickens. In the fall, Poppie hunted the big Canada geese that were migrating south. If they had extra meat, they preserved it with salt.

Mama and Poppie always welcomed others to share their meals. Settlers dropping in on each other at mealtime usually brought along food, but bachelor neighbors, travelers on their way past, or hired help were always invited to eat with the family. Most settlers were experts at stretching their food for unexpected guests.

Preparing food took the most of Mama's time, but her hardest job was washing clothes, which took one whole day every week. If the pond was dry, the water had to come from the barrels. She needed a good fire in the stove to heat the water, no matter how hot the weather might be. Then she scrubbed each piece on a washboard with homemade soap. Baby diapers and Poppie's work clothes were always the hardest to get clean. Next she rinsed each piece in another tub, wrung out the excess water, and hung each piece outside to dry, draping it over bushes and the grass. If the weather was rainy, she spread the clothes around the soddy.

The next day she would heat up the heavy irons on the stove and press the finer clothes—slips, blouses, and dresses—starching them first. Mama made her own starch, which required boiling grated potatoes and skimming off the top until the starch that was left settled to the bottom of the pot. This was gathered and dried, then mixed with water to form a paste. Starching sunbonnets was a big job. The brims had to be perfectly stiff or they would hang over the wearer's eyes.

Mama felt lucky to have a sewing machine to help make and mend clothes. She sat at the machine for hours, treadling away with her feet. Keeping Grace neatly dressed was difficult. "Florry outgrew her clothes before she wore them out, but I tore mine off of me faster than Mama could sew them up," Grace recalled. Mama finally made Grace denim overalls and a denim jacket. Grace was thrilled.

She was wearing her overalls one fall day when a crew of neighbors, who traveled from farm to farm to help one another harvest their wheat, arrived to help Poppie with his first wheat crop. One of the neighbors owned a threshing machine that would separate the grain from the straw much faster than it could be separated by hand. Working together, the farmers would cut the grain in a field and then feed it into the machine, which was powered by teams of horses pulling it in a circle. Boys eight or older helped with the threshing, while girls that age worked in the kitchen and took water to the threshers.

Grace and Florry were too young to help, but they loved to watch. One day Grace got too close to the machine and a farmer yelled, "'Hey! Get that little boy outta here before he gets hurted.'" She cried indignantly, "'I'm not a boy, I'm a girl!'" But when Grace complained to her mother, Mama just gave her an "I told you so" expression.

Cloth was expensive, and Mama mended and patched every piece

Boys helped bring in the crops.

of clothing until it was good only for scraps. Even those were used for household chores or to make rag rugs. Mama saved the best scraps for quilts. Her stitches were straight and even, and Grace hoped someday she could sew that well.

Another of Mama's jobs was supervising the family's once-a-week baths. When water was scarce, most pioneers did not take regular baths, but Mama insisted on them. She heated the water, poured it into the big tub she kept behind the stove, and then scrubbed the girls with homemade soap. All three used the same tub of water. In between baths, the family washed up using a basin.

One of Mama's daily chores was to empty and rinse the chamber pot, a deep porcelain bowl with a cover. The family used it to go to the bathroom in during the night or when the weather was bad and they could not go outside to the outhouse.

When pioneers first moved to their claims, women usually insisted on proper privies as soon as possible. The pioneers would dig a deep hole, construct a foundation, often from rocks, and then place a tiny wood or sod building over it. Many had a bench with holes of several sizes. Settlers often whitewashed the walls to make the privies light and clean, and kept mail-order catalogs there for reading. Pages from the catalogs were also used as toilet paper. So were corncobs and scraps of fabric.

Where to go to the bathroom was a problem for travelers, especially if there were no trees to offer privacy. Women and older girls would shield each other with their skirts.

One day when she went to town with Poppie, Grace was so excited about the trip that she forgot to ask Mama where she could go to the bathroom. By the time Poppie was done with his errands and they were ready to leave, Grace needed to go so badly she thought she was going to pop. On their way out of town, Poppie asked her if she had had a good time. "I began to howl like a puppy that's had its tail stepped on," remembered Grace. Poppie understood then, and stopped the wagon so she could get out and find a place to relieve herself.

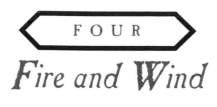

FOUR

Fire and Wind

During the fall, Grace and Florry played outside whenever they could. Their favorite place was the old buffalo trail that wound over the prairie and out of sight from the house. Their cat liked to go with them. Sometimes they found tiny shells in the soil and would bring them home to Mama. She explained how, millions of years ago, glaciers covered the land. When they melted, they created a sea. That's where the shells had come from.

Later Grace learned that the Midwest was dry because the Rocky Mountains in Colorado blocked moisture blowing inland from the Pacific Ocean. Nebraska was one of the driest Midwest states. The few trees grew mostly along the rivers. Rainfall also affected how tall the grass grew. Travelers going west noticed that the closer they got to the Rocky Mountains, the shorter the grass was. "Shortgrass" grew only six to twelve inches tall. On the eastern side of the Midwest, known as the "tallgrass" prairie, native grasses got enough rain to grow six to twelve *feet* in height. In the shortgrass area where the McCances lived, Poppie planted types of wheat and corn that needed little rainfall. His crops still had to have *some* rain, however, and like all farmers he kept one eye on the weather.

The weather was always a concern. Hailstorms could pound crops to pieces in a matter of minutes, and injure or kill birds and animals. Hailstones even killed people caught without shelter. Lightning was another danger. Grace once saw a horse that had been killed by lightning. When the weather was dry, lightning, a spark from a campfire, or a gun discharge could start prairie fires, and the wind would spread them.

Settlers banded together to fight the fires. Sometimes they tried setting backfires—burning a strip of land in the fire's path so that when the fire reached the strip, it either burned out or turned in a different direction. Like every settler, Poppie tried to keep firebreaks—grassless ditches the fires could not cross—plowed around his land. But sometimes, if prairie fires were moving fast enough, they could jump firebreaks and be stopped only by a river or a creek.

Grace never forgot her first prairie fire. As soon as Poppie saw

*As this drawing from **Harper's Weekly** shows, the settlers fought fires without fire trucks, hoses, or—many times—even water.*

smoke in the far hills, he took off in the wagon with a barrel of water to help fight it. Mama, Florry, and Grace watched all morning as the fire drew closer to their land. Grace was frightened.

Mama told the girls that if the fire jumped the firebreak they would run to the middle of the big bare field where the fire would have nothing to burn and would either go around them or die out. When the flames reached the firebreaks, Grace was ready to run. Then she saw that the fire was going out. When Poppie finally came home, his clothes and skin were black from soot.

A few months after the fire, a rainstorm struck the homestead. The howling of the wind woke everyone up. Suddenly "the darkness, black and thick as velvet, was ripped apart by a terrible blue flash of lightning," Grace remembered. "Then there was a cracking, tearing sound, and the soddy seemed to quiver."

The noise was the roof being torn off the kitchen. When the storm finally stopped, the house was "a sorry-looking mess. Every last thing had blown off the walls, and all Mama's little shelves, brackets, whatnots, and pictures were either smashed to bits or gone entirely." Grace remembered that "Mama went around in a kind of a daze, picking some of her torn and broken things out of the hash on the floor and sweeping out the worst of the mud. The hot sun was pouring down on our heads when Poppie, hard put to keep a cheerful expression on his face, offered thanks for the cornmeal mush and fried eggs we finally sat down to."

The girls helped Mama carry water to clean up. Poppie hunted for roof boards that had blown away and set to work rebuilding the roof. Grace and her mother walked through the fields looking for their belongings. They "found half of the marriage certificate, but no part of the frame or glass. Just that half, ripped from the rest, its doves and cupids hardly stained by the mud and rain."

Storms could destroy a pioneer family's house and fields.

Still, Poppie was not discouraged. Like most farmers, he lived on hope, always convinced that the next year would be better.

When early November's chill made it too cold to play outside, Grace and Florry gathered up their cob dolls and settled into the sod house for the winter. "Flour sacks full of beans and fried corn hung in the kitchen corner that winter, and heaps of onions, turnips, pumpkins, cabbage, and potatoes filled the cellar cave."

Just before Thanksgiving, Poppie came home from one of his weekly trips to town with three barrels in the back of the wagon. They had come by railroad from Grandma and Grandpa Blaine, Mama's parents back in Missouri. Grace and Florry and even little Stella were almost beside themselves with excitement when Poppie started to pry off the lids.

The first one was filled with molasses to sweeten their cereal and Mama's baked goods. The second was full of red apples from Grandpa Blaine's orchard behind the big white house. Grace saw the faraway look in Mama's eyes when she took one and held it in her hands.

The third barrel was the best. First they pulled out bags of black walnuts from Grandpa's nut trees and sweet potatoes from his garden. Then came Grandma's bundles. One contained a dress length of new calico fabric for Mama and each of the girls. The other held clothes from Mama's younger sister, Aunt Ollie, who always wore the latest styles. She had sent along jackets, dresses, and petticoats she did not want anymore.

Mama laid everything out on the bed, and Grace and Florry gazed at the lovely garments. Mama would make over the clothes so the girls would have new outfits. And she promised to have their new calico dresses made in time for Christmas dinner.

That first Christmas, Mama and Poppie could not afford any presents, but Poppie cut down a little wild plum bush and Grace and Florry decorated it with paper chains and strings of popcorn. All three girls wore their new dresses when the neighbors came to feast on a roast turkey dinner. Grace's only complaint was that the table was not big enough. She and Florry and the neighbors' children had to wait until the adults finished at "first table" before it was their turn to eat. "While hard knots of hunger grew and grew inside us, we had to sit back, smelling the good smells, and hoping there would be enough of everything left for us," she recalled. "Homestead children had to put up with a lot of hard things, but one of the hardest was waiting for second table."

FIVE

Sunup to Sundown

Spring came again, and the prairie turned soft green. Grace was now four and lingered outside. "The first day of going barefoot was almost as good as Christmas, or the Fourth of July," she recalled. "There is almost no describing it; the good feeling to tender, bare soles of cushiony new buffalo grass, or of the fine, warm dust of a cow trail."

Everything on the homestead was humming and growing. The horse gave birth to a colt. Pearlie the cow had a calf. Little chicks followed the fussy old turkey hens. Poppie planted his wheat, and then had to use his shotgun to fight off flocks of geese flying north that kept stealing the precious seeds. Mama planted her garden again, a bigger one this year. "Poppie said, for the hundredth time, that he had never seen such a land as this, so rich, so fertile. But Mama said only that she wished we had a well in our own yard."

Poppie kept after the well men, but they had so much business from all the new homesteaders in the area that they raised their rates. Poppie said he and Mama did not have enough money. He would have to keep hauling water until he could dig the well himself.

Their second year on the prairie passed much as the first. Grace and Florry still begged to go whenever Poppie loaded up the water barrels. If Mama would relent, "we had fun, jouncing along in the wagon and singing with Poppie above the rattle and bang of the empty barrels. . . . When we pulled up at the well, our neighbor, Mrs. Totten, would come out to visit with us while Poppie filled the barrels, or maybe she would take us to the house with her."

The Tottens were only a few miles away, but Mama still felt as if she lived in the middle of nowhere. That changed when the Yoders, who had been the McCances' neighbors in Missouri, took a claim nearby. "Their arrival made Mama happier than anything that had happened since we came to Nebraska," Grace realized.

On Mama's birthday in April, she decided the family should visit the Yoders since their son's birthday was the same day. Mama began preparing food to take with them. Grace and Florry did their chores and took baths, put on their best petticoats, and tried to stand still while Mama braided their long hair. Then Mama brushed her own hair and arranged it stylishly on her head. Just as they all finished dressing, Mama glanced out the window and cried, "'Merciful heavens, there's the Yoders, the whole family, and look at this house!'"

Grace and Florry looked—at a tub of cold dirty bathwater, clothes strewn everywhere, and the kitchen not yet tidied from breakfast. While Mama hurriedly picked up, Grace and Florry grabbed the bath basin and dragged it outside, just as their unexpected guests came to the door. They had brought a birthday dinner for Mama and their son, all ready to eat.

The homesteaders settling around the McCances were mostly Swedish immigrants. When the farmers gathered together to help harvest one another's wheat crops, Poppie, whose ancestors were Scottish and Irish, missed out on most of the conversation, which was in Swedish.

Immigrants who settled in the Midwest usually came for the rich

Immigrants, like this French family who pioneered in Kansas, played an important role in helping to settle the Midwest.

farmland. In the countries they left behind, they either could not afford to own land or were not allowed to. Some also came to find religious freedom, to escape paying unfair taxes, or to avoid serving in the military. So many Germans settled in Kansas during the 1860s and 1870s that one tribe of Kansas Indians spoke German as a second language instead of English. In 1870, over half of Nebraska's population was made up of foreign-born immigrants and their American-born children.

Like Poppie, many people born in the United States also wanted to homestead. Some had lost their homes in the Civil War or thought the

East was getting too crowded. Freed slaves came because they wanted to leave the South, and homesteading was a way they could own land. Sometimes freed slaves established a community, such as the little Kansas town of Nicodemus.

Most homesteaders were poor. Children were often barefoot because they owned no shoes. One child remembered that his parents used kegs for chairs during family meals and the children stood. Before they had those kegs, they sat on pumpkins.

Everyone worked six days a week, including small children. Three-year-olds could act as human scarecrows to chase grain-eating birds out of the fields and help gather chips for fuel. Four-year-olds ran errands, took water to field-workers, and gathered eggs. Five-year-olds helped break up clods in the fields, pull weeds, feed the cookstove, milk cows, and even plow. One six-year-old boy sent to find stray cattle was gone several days before his father set out to search for him and found him not far from home, returning with the lost cows.

Grace and Florry had always helped out. When Grace was five and Florry was seven, they were given a new chore: looking for turkey nests. When chicken and turkey hens turned "broody" in the spring, they stopped laying for several weeks so they could sit on one batch of eggs long enough for them to hatch into baby chicks. But they often laid their eggs far from home, where skunks and snakes could get them and where coyotes could kill the hens. The girls' job was to find the nests and get the hens to "brood" them back at the stable. Grace recalled, "The hens would stroll the prairie for hours, acting as if they had nowhere to go and nothing to do. Sometimes we sat watching a hen for a solid half day, and then somehow missed her when she slipped, like the shadow of a cloud, into some patch of brush or tall grass and disappeared."

In the fall of 1887, Poppie bought a small herd of cattle. Since

*E*ven very young pioneer children helped feed animals, milk cows,
and do other chores.

there were no boys in the family, he called on five-year-old Grace,
nicknaming her Pete because she would be doing work usually done
by a boy. He said, "'You'll have to be my herd boy now, Pete. Mommie
needs Florry to help her in the house and you'll have to do it all alone.
Think you can?'" Grace was thrilled. She disliked housework and preferred to work outdoors.

Her job was to drive the cattle to the fields in the morning, stay with them all day, and bring them home in the evening. Herding would have gone fine, had it not been for one mean-tempered heifer who constantly threatened Grace with her sharp horns. Grace had to carry a stout stick to protect herself. One evening the cows turned contrary and wanted to stay inside the cave they had created in the big haystack: "No matter how much I ran and yelled and whacked, they outran me and dodged back into the cave. Finally, I pushed past them into the hole and began pounding on their heads with my stick. The older cows gave up and backed out together, leaving me suddenly face-to-face with the long-nosed, ornery heifer."

As the heifer rushed her, Grace flattened herself against the hay, but the heifer gouged a deep cut from her hip to armpit. As much as it hurt, Grace got the cows home, even the heifer. When she was finally in the house, she burst into tears. Mama cared for her, then told Poppie he had to get rid of the heifer or Grace could no longer herd. Poppie said he would sell the heifer the next time he went to town. In the meantime, he would keep her in the corral.

A few days later, when Grace was in the barn helping with the milking, she heard a snort behind her. She whirled around and saw the heifer, head down, coming straight for her. Grace made a mad dash, ducking under one of the cows and rolling under the barbed-wire fence. She was unhurt, but she was wearing her favorite calico dress and ripped it so badly it was ruined. That made her cry more than the scare. Poppie sold the heifer in town the next day.

SIX

Pioneer Women

During the long hours herding cattle, Grace had no one to talk to and nothing to do with her hands. She was bored. One evening as she watched Mama piecing together squares of calico for a quilt top, she asked for some pieces of cloth to sew while she was herding. Mama said she was too young, but Grace promised to do a good job. Mama finally said she could have four little squares to stitch together. "'But you'll have to do neat work and fasten the ends of your thread good,' she said, 'for I can't afford to waste thread and pieces on you if you don't.'"

Grace stitched carefully so that her mother would give her more fabric. "I knew that Mama's needlework was extra fine, and that it wouldn't be easy to learn to sew as well as she did. But it was during those days, when I worked so hard to keep my stitches even and the block corners matched, that I began to dream of the time when I could make quilts even finer than Mama's, finer than any others in the world."

Grace never complained to Mama about herding. She knew her mother wanted her to be ladylike and not do outside work. Pioneer daughters often clashed with their more genteel mothers about their behavior. Many mother-daughter battles focused on the sunbonnet.

Women formed sewing circles so they could do their needlework while visiting with one another.

Little girls would throw off the hot, awkward headgear. Those with light skin would tan and freckle, upsetting their mothers who believed, as did other white-skinned American women at that time, that a smooth untanned face was a sign of beauty. Mama insisted on sunbonnets. Florry always kept hers on and did not mind when Mama rubbed buttermilk on her cheeks to soften her skin. Grace wore her hat only to please her mother—in spite of buttermilk and bonnets, her skin still turned brown.

Some homesteading women wore corsets and high-heeled shoes while they worked. Not Mama. She liked to look stylish, but she was also practical. She always wore an apron over her loose black dresses, which helped keep them clean. She could wash and iron an apron more easily than a dress. And aprons were useful. She could wipe her hands on them, take hold of a hot pan, dry a dish, and gather eggs by holding the corners to create a carryall.

Pioneer women preferred sturdy calico dresses for everyday wear, but many still liked to know what was fashionable. They subscribed to women's magazines like *Godey's Lady's Book* and received mail-order catalogs like Montgomery Ward's that showed the latest styles. Many were clever at sewing copies of them to wear for special occasions and for church.

Even though they lived in primitive houses, pioneer women were also interested in home decorating. They brought flower seeds, feather pillows, quilts, and lace tablecloths from their former homes. They copied the popular styles of the day, such as the Victorian preference for covering every surface with a different pattern. They also enjoyed reading and rereading works of classical literature they had brought with them. The first baby born in a soddy near Dodge City, Kansas, was named Childe Harold after a character in a poem by Lord Byron. Most women were determined to not give in to the roughness of their lives. Some served every meal on the good china they had brought west with them. They trained their children to use proper table manners and allowed no swear words.

Still, Mama and other pioneer women lived very differently from their own mothers. When necessary, they helped their husbands in the fields and barns. When husbands took outside jobs, women often did all the chores and cared for the crops. Women sometimes took outside jobs as well, working as cooks, housekeepers, seamstresses, and school-teachers.

Women started schools, churches, libraries, and missionary societies, and they helped their neighbors. The Midwest could not have been settled without them; yet women were usually viewed as "helping out" their husbands. Within the family, they were expected to obey the men. Pioneer life was physically hard on them. A twenty-nine-year-old pioneer wrote in a letter, "I am a very old woman. My face is thin, sunken, and wrinkled, my hands bony, withered, and hard."

As an adult, Grace observed, "Early marriages, big families, and years of hard work turned most of the women I knew old long before middle age." She saw this with her mother. Mama was never very strong, and having babies was hard on her. Like most women at that time, however, she probably knew nothing about how to plan the number of children she wanted. She was so modest about the human body that Grace figured "she probably never in her life saw all of her own body at once"—which would have been typical of women in the late 1800s. She would not have discussed family planning with a doctor, nor would she have discussed the facts of life with her daughters. Like many other children, Grace and her sisters had to figure out for themselves where babies came from. One pioneer girl who was playing house with her brothers secretly slipped a baby doll into the doll bed. "My little brothers were so surprised to see an addition to the family. 'Just like grown-ups,'" she explained. "'You just wake up some morning and there's a new baby.'"

And one morning Grace and Florry and Stella woke up to find they had a new sister lying next to Mama. Although the girls were disappointed she was not the brother they wanted, they were still very pleased with her. But they were surprised, because they had not known the baby was expected. Mama always wore loose-fitting dresses, so they had not noticed anything. Mama said their new sister would be named Florence Ethel, but right away they all started calling her Dovey because Mama said the little noises she made were like the cooing sounds of a dove.

When Dovey was just a few days old and Mama was still bedfast, a terrible summer storm blew in. Poppie was watching it from a window when he saw lightning strike a haystack by the barn, setting the hay on fire. They ran outside to put out the blaze. As they returned to the house, they saw smoke coming from the bedroom. Poppie ran into the smoke-filled room and quickly doused a little fire that had started when a candle had fallen over. Mama was fighting for breath. They had come just in time: "Mama . . . was almost unconscious and the baby had nearly quit breathing."

Soon after that, Grandma McCance, Poppie's mother, came to help out. Grandma had raised nine children. She was feeling at loose ends on her farm in Missouri. This was her first visit to Nebraska, and she liked it. She told Poppie that if he could get a good farm for her nearby, she would move. Grace and Florry thought that would be wonderful. They loved Grandma McCance, who was little and wiry and always busy with something. By the time Grandma left, she had been there a month, and they were sorry to see her go.

A week later a letter arrived from Grandma Blaine announcing that *she* was coming for a visit. This was a different matter. "Mama held the letter in her hand a long time, a stricken look on her face." She was still weak, so Poppie arranged for a hired girl to help out until Mama was satisfied that the house was as clean as it could possibly be. Everyone helped. "The whitewashing, scrubbing, and dusting went on right up to the minute Poppie left for Cozad to meet the train." Then Mama "turned on Florry, Stella, and me and scrubbed us almost to the quick—as if she hoped to wash off our sunburn and scratches—and hustled us into clean clothes from the skin out."

Grandma Blaine's visit was hard on Mama. She wanted her mother to think well of her life. "Poor Mama," Grace said later. "She knew how raw and bare our prairie home would seem to her mother. But Florry and I, scarcely remembering anything different, or better, were proud to show Grandma around. And Grandma, rustling and dainty in her silk dress and many petticoats, smiled at us and smoothed our wind-roughened hair with gentle fingers."

Late that summer, after Grandma Blaine was gone and Mama felt better, Poppie finally started the well. The best location would require carrying water uphill, but nobody cared. "Mama said that just having a well on the place, after three years of hauling water and never having enough to take more than a spit bath in, would seem heavenly," Grace recalled.

Every day that Poppie worked on the well, they worried about him. They had heard stories about two neighbors who had been killed while digging their wells. One had fallen into the well shaft; the other died in a cave-in. Poppie worked on the well whenever he could, stopping only to take care of farm duties and to haul water. A neighbor helped. One man climbed into the hole to dig while the other pulled up buckets filled with dirt. As they dug, they built a wood casing to keep the well shaft from collapsing.

On a great day in September, they struck water at a depth of one hundred fifty feet—about the distance from the roof to the basement of a thirteen-story building. Poppie hitched up Old Peg, the mule, to the pulley, and she did the work of a windmill, pulling water buckets to the surface, where Poppie could empty them into a water tank for the livestock or into the water barrel for the house. Grace noted, "Old Peg was the first automatic power we ever owned."

During the heat of the summer when water was scarce, the family could look outside on moonlit nights and see wild animals drinking from the water tank. Later Poppie built a windmill, which could lift hundreds of gallons of water a day. But windmills did more than harness the wind. These tall structures also helped people locate a specific homestead. Since trees were scarce and the base of the windmill

Windmills built over wells pumped water to the surface and also showed travelers where houses were located.

was cool and shady, it was a favorite spot for summer picnics. Nobody minded the thumps and squeaks the windmill made, for those noises represented life-giving water.

The well changed everything for the McCances. No more hauling barrels of water. No more sharing bathwater. No more worrying if there would be enough water to put out fires.

That first day with water, Mama took a long drink of the delicious, cold liquid—and then began scrubbing everything in sight. Grace was not a bit surprised when she started with the children's dirty faces.

SEVEN

Blizzards and Grasshoppers

From the time Grace was six until she was ten, the McCance family knew mostly happy times. Two more children joined the family. Nellie was born in 1889 when Grace was seven. Unlike her four brown-eyed sisters, this little one had blue eyes.

Mama was bedfast for a month, trying to recover her strength, but she got up the day she realized the temporary hired girl had given head lice to all the children. Mama fired her and went to work. She whacked off the children's braids and went over their heads several times with a fine-tooth comb dipped in kerosene. Florry was upset at this unexpected haircut, but Grace was delighted: "I had always begrudged every minute that it took to comb and plait my long, heavy braids, and I loved the feel of my new, short, 'boy' haircut."

The other new family member was Maud Elsie, born in 1892. She had black hair and brown eyes like Grace, who reported: "She was a plump, good baby and Mama called her 'Precious,' a pet name the rest of us had shortened to 'Presh' by the time she could sit alone." This time it took Mama several months to recover her health.

Grandma McCance moved nearby, bringing with her Poppie's brother John; his youngest sisters, Bell and Hester; and Aunt Dicy. The girls loved having their relatives near them. Grace was especially fond of Aunt Bell, who often gave her bundles of scraps to use for quilt pieces.

Aunt Dicy was an orphan who had grown up with Grandma McCance. Her mother had been "a poor crazy woman," the family said, and Dicy was "simple" like a small child. She sang sad songs. According to Grace, "We loved Aunt Dicy, too, although she was old and anything but pretty, having long ago lost all her teeth and most of her hair."

Poppie and Uncle John built a five-room shingle-roof sod house for Grandma, completing it to her specifications. Grace remembered, "Mama said that Grandma, being the boss in her household, got her house built the way she wanted it; while women with husbands had to put up with whatever their menfolk thought was the cheapest and the quickest."

Of all the things that happened to Grace between her sixth and tenth birthdays, the hardest was having to move. She had just turned eight when Poppie bought a nearby homestead with better land for crops and grazing. It was closer to town and closer to Grandma McCance. Also, the sod house on it was bigger, and there was a well right by the kitchen door. The house even had a parlor for Mama, although it would have to double as a bedroom.

At the new place, Poppie's first harvests were bountiful, and crop prices were good. He built a granary, started an orchard, and added other improvements to the property. He also bought Mama a washing machine. Though it required pushing a handle back and forth to operate the clothes scrubber, it was better than hand-scrubbing clothes on a washboard and it took much less time. Poppie also bought a new stove and sewing machine, and, best of all, a beautiful wagon with padded leather seats "that were soft as air."

Just as she had at the old place, Grace soon knew every inch of the

A good harvest was cause for rejoicing.

new land. She found some buffalo bones and even a few Indian arrow-heads, but the only time she saw Indians was at celebrations in town when they would come from the reservation where they lived. The railroad, the government, and settlers had already pushed the Indians aside.

Grace sometimes wondered how Indians living in teepees had withstood Nebraska's harsh winter, always the most dangerous season. Out on the open prairie, the cold and the wind could kill, especially if people or animals could not find shelter. Several days of heavy snow could bury fuel and all food for livestock.

Grace never forgot the blizzard that occurred January 12, 1888. Luckily everyone was home and the family stayed snug and safe. But the storm brought great suffering throughout the Midwest. Hundreds of people and thousands of animals died. Many people lost fingers, toes, hands, and feet to frostbite.

The blizzard of '88 came to be known as the Schoolchildren's

When cattle were caught in a blizzard, they sometimes starved or froze to death.

Blizzard, since many children were in school when it struck. Some had not even worn coats that warm winter day. Then the wind changed suddenly and clouds came rolling in like thick bales of cotton, driving heavy snow in their wake. Quickly the weather turned freezing cold. Farmers in the fields struggled to get back to their houses. Animals suffocated or froze under the raging snow.

Schoolhouses were usually not built very well and often had little fuel on hand. Most schoolteachers were teenage girls. Some became frantic. They had to decide whether to stay in the schoolhouse overnight, knowing they might freeze, or try to get the children home without getting lost. Many who survived the night in their schools burned the desks to stay warm.

The storm was most dangerous on open prairie, but some townspeople froze to death when they got caught outside in the storm's whiteout. The newspapers reported that in Hastings, Nebraska, a blind college professor was the hero of the blizzard. He did not become disoriented in the storm as sighted people did, so he was able to get to the local school. He had the children form a human chain and managed to get every child safely home.

The only other event Grace ever heard of that was as terrible as the Blizzard of '88 was the grasshopper infestation of 1874, before she was born. Grasshoppers were one of the few living things she disliked. There were always some around, and they were a slimy nuisance, leaving stains on everything they touched and eating holes through everything they landed on.

People said that in 1874 the grasshoppers were like a biblical plague. Millions came, blocking the light of the sun and stripping a farm bare in a matter of hours. They ate crops, gardens, stored food, clothing, bedding, leaves, bark, grass, fences, plow handles, woodwork, and furniture. Their dead bodies soured well water for weeks. Trains stopped running when the tracks became greasy from grasshopper bodies piled six inches deep. Many farmers were ruined and had to move away or take jobs in town.

Grace thought about the grasshopper plague when she saw the chickens eating them, particularly the big white rooster who was her special pet for a time. "He was so friendly and seemed to like me so much, and I took to carrying him with me while I herded," she recalled. "After an hour or so on the prairie he'd have his craw so full of grasshoppers he could hardly see over it, and then he'd sit beside me and visit, clucking and chirping at a great rate as long as I'd answer him.

"He was a very polite chicken that way."

EIGHT

Sociable Settlers

The rooster was just one of the pets Grace had as a child. Along with Old Tom the cat, Old Peg the mule, and Pearlie the cow, she also had several herd dogs who helped her move the cows along, including one dog that was killed by a rattlesnake. The dog she had the longest was Rover. He was always running, digging, or "wearing himself out piling up cats."

Whenever there were kittens around, Rover seemed to think it was his job to keep them in a pile in the orchard. Grace remembered, "He worked so hard at it, carrying one kitten after another to the pile, but while he was going after the last two the first two would be scooting back to the house. Poppie said it looked like he'd learn, after a while, that piling up cats paid off about as fast as pouring water in a basket with a sieve."

Grace's affection for the prairie deepened during those years between her sixth and tenth birthdays. When she and Florry started going to the country school three miles from home, Grace thought "the long walks through the dewy mornings and sunny afternoons were pure pleasure." She noticed every bird, plant, and animal. Her favorite place was the prairie dog town where "sassy prairie dogs bounced and chattered at us before diving headfirst into their holes." The girls felt protective of the little critters.

"One cool morning we came onto a whopping big bull snake just sliding into a hole in the dog town," Grace said. "We grabbed his rear half and pulled, but he had such a purchase on the sides of the hole that our hands kept slipping on his smooth skin. About to lose him, we tried wrapping our hands in the skirts of the long capes we wore. It was easy, then, to yank him out on the prairie, where we 'stomped' him to death." The girls were proud of what they had done, but Poppie scolded them. Bull snakes helped the farmers by eating mice and other rodents who ate crops, he said.

Grace's walks by the prairie dog town ended after only a few weeks because Poppie needed her at home. So Florry walked by herself and Grace went back to herding, milking, and fieldwork. For several years, her schooling was sporadic, depending on whether Poppie needed her to be his "boy."

Fieldwork was the worst because of the dust, bugs, mud, and heat. The mules could be stubborn, and she always returned home exhausted and filthy. By comparison, herding was easy. Grace had time to stitch her quilt squares and to wish that someday she would make the finest quilts in the world. She liked to lie in the grass and daydream as she watched the clouds.

Not going to school meant she was never around anyone except her family. Fortunately, Poppie liked to socialize and Grace could usually talk him into taking her to evening or weekend events at the church or schoolhouse. Most country people used any excuse for a get-together. They would hold a "bee" to do everything from building a barn for an ailing neighbor to helping one another harvest crops, turning work into fun.

At a husking bee, contestants moved through a cornfield row by row, removing husks from the corn, plucking the ears from the stalks, and then throwing them into the waiting wagon, competing to see who could work the fastest. When young people helped husk, there was a tradition that if a boy found a red ear of corn, he could kiss the girl next to him in line. Sometimes boys smuggled red ears from home and then "found" them so they could kiss their favorite girl.

Women got together for quilting bees. While they exchanged scraps of fabric and worked together to attach quilt bottoms and tops, they visited. Husbands often came along and played horseshoes and checkers and talked with one another about their families, their crops, and the weather. Neighbors also took turns hosting taffy pulls, fish fries, barn dances, masquerades, and balls.

Holidays were always times of celebration. For Christmas, families decorated little trees or even tumbleweeds with nuts, berries, popcorn, candles, candy, and homemade ornaments. Santa almost always brought something—at least a piece of fruit and a homemade toy. One pioneer child remembered, "Mother made our Christmas gifts. A matchbox covered with pretty paper and decorated with pictures from the seed catalog was one of my treasured gifts. Another was a cardboard star covered with the tinfoil from a tea package."

After their first Christmas with no gifts, Mama and Poppie were able to use the money from selling Mama's turkeys to buy Christmas presents. Mostly gifts were practical—overshoes, mittens, and winter hats. But there would be some special items, too, like hair ribbons and candy.

Grace liked the Fourth of July even better than Christmas. Many homestead children were lucky if they could go to town six times a year, but a trip July 4th was the one they begged hardest for. Cozad always held a big celebration, and Grace loved it. Everyone dressed up, and Mama made the girls new dresses. The day's activities included a

This 1889 Fourth of July celebration included costumes and a parade.

parade through the streets, with the town band leading a procession of buggies, surreys, carriages, and farm machinery. Grace especially liked seeing the workhorses from the local farms prance past.

The parade was followed by footraces, a tug-of-war, and the greased pole climb. For this event, the first boy who could climb to the top of the slippery fourteen-foot pole won the silver dollar at the top. At noon, everyone unpacked their picnic baskets at the pavilion in the park. Mama always brought her special five-layer cake, and the McCances joined their neighbors, the Yoders, and whatever relatives had come, and they all ate until they were stuffed. After lunch, there were songs, speeches, and patriotic addresses.

Then came the event Grace loved best of all—the water fight. Two teams of volunteer firefighters squirted each other with hoses until one side gave up. By then, "the bystanders were a whole lot wetter than the fighters." The day ended with fireworks.

Now that they lived closer to town, Poppie was able to join a baseball team in Cozad. One day he shot an antelope and used the hide to make a chest protector for the team's catcher. Grace liked to go along when Poppie had a game. Sometimes there would be an outdoor band concert they could attend afterward. Town picnics, debates, musical recitals, card parties—something was always going on.

Occasionally the family attended a religious revival in order to hear a visiting preacher. People would come from all over to socialize and pray together, sometimes for several days at a time. Religion was important to many settlers. The first church services on the prairie were held in homes or at the schoolhouse. People of any religion were

The McCance family reunion, 1892: Mama and Poppie are standing to the far right. In front of them are babies Elsie and

welcome. The first ministers were usually "traveling preachers" who served several churches, reaching them by horseback and relying on the hospitality of church members for room and board.

Once churches were built, they became social as well as religious centers. Settlers gathered for Sunday services and Sunday school, weddings, funerals, baptisms, socials, suppers, missionary societies, and choir practices. The McCances attended church and Sunday school whenever they could.

Grandma McCance liked family get-togethers. The summer of 1892, when relatives came to visit from Missouri, she hired a photographer. Grace was ten that year, and she and all five of her sisters had whooping cough, but everyone came over to Mama and Poppie's soddy anyway. Grace said, "Grandma and Aunt Dicy, in their good black dresses, looked as smooth and shiny as a pair of jet buttons, and

Nellie. Seated to the far right are (left to right) Stella, Florry, Grace, and Ethel.

it seemed like Sunday, with all of us standing around in our best clothes, waiting for the photographer to come from Cozad." Mama brought her two canary cages outside to be in the picture. Settlers often included their prized possessions in photographs, from sewing machines to livestock to buggies. They wanted to show that even if they lived in dirt houses, they were civilized, and in some instances even prosperous.

In the 1800s, people usually did not smile in photographs. Such an important occasion required a serious face. Also, for the photographer to get the exposure right, people had to sit still for a long time. Another reason there were few smiles was that most people had bad teeth and wanted to hide them. And even in the heat of summer, people wore their Sunday best, which was usually heavy clothing. By the time the picture was taken, they were in no mood to smile.

That summer was a hot one. Grace would longingly eye the cold-water tank by the windmill when she came in from the fields, feeling as if she were cooked alive in the high-necked, long-sleeved dress Mama insisted she wear. When she asked if she and her sisters could swim to cool off, Mama was shocked: "We told her we'd wear old dresses while we were in the water, but she still said no, that we were getting too big to strip off that near naked where Poppie or someone might see us."

One scorching day when Mama left for town with Poppie, taking the two youngest girls with them, Grace convinced Florry, Stella, and Dovey that they could go swimming as long as they watched the road to make sure no one saw them. They climbed into the tank and were soon playing and splashing in the cool water.

Then Grace sat on a wasp and her sisters were laughing so hard at the fuss she made that none of them thought to watch the road. They looked up just as a wagon went by, and saw "the shocked faces of three ladies, and a man rocking back and forth on the front seat and laughing so hard his shoulders shook. We were a sad bunch of girls all the rest of that afternoon, for we knew Mama would find out about it someway, and we knew we'd 'catch it' when she did."

Even so, Grace was not sorry they had taken that wonderful swim.

NINE

The Storm

The year 1892 ended with two weddings, Aunt Bell's and then Uncle John's. Grace turned eleven the following spring and she found herself thinking about her own future. She could feel her body changing and maturing. Her daydreams were changing, too. She had seen a picture in her schoolbook of a cowboy, and it had fired her imagination. She had never seen a real cowboy—all the boys she knew were the sons of homesteaders who rode farm horses. But in her dreams, a cowboy on a fine horse would come galloping up to her. She would get onto the horse he was leading and would ride off to help look after his cattle.

"At the time there was no romance in my dream," Grace recalled. What mattered was the horse and saddle. With a saddle, she could ride faster and farther than she could riding bareback, but saddles were expensive and she doubted she would ever be able to afford one. She had no money of her own. Her parents did not pay her for the work she did, nor did she expect them to.

Everything was going well for the McCances that summer, Grace remembered. There had been plenty of rain, so the crops were looking good. "Poppie and the neighbors talked of replacing sod buildings with frame before long, and of buying more land and livestock, or new machinery and furniture." The orchard was thriving. Poppie said the wheat would pay off the farm debts. He planned to increase the number of pigs they were raising and talked about getting a hired man to help with the work so Grace could go to school full-time. Crop prices were high, and Mama's chickens and turkeys were selling well. Cozad was booming, and so was North Platte, the nearest "big" town. Up and down the valley, prosperity was in the air.

Then everything began to change.

In early August, the "hot winds began to blow. In other summers we had had the hot winds for a day or two—but now they blew on and on without letup. Day by day the corn shriveled until, by the end of the month, the stalks stood white and lifeless. The prairie turned brown and brittle and the land seemed to pant for breath under the burning sun."

Poppie had to put his plans on hold. Since there would be no harvest, he had no fieldwork. He took over the herding and sent Grace to school all day; he figured "you had to expect a bad year now and then." Although money would be tight, the sale of Mama's fat turkeys would get them through the winter.

But one cold evening in December, the turkeys did not come home to roost. Mama was worried that coyotes had gotten them. The next day they learned that the turkeys had strayed to another farm. The neighbor brought them back, reporting that he and his wife had not noticed they had more turkeys than usual when they started preparing them for market: "'I told the ole lady we was aputtin' too many gobblers in the barr'l, so we counted up, and, sure enough, we had about twict too many. I've brung you back what gobblers 're left, and yer hens, and enough of ourn to make up fer what we killed of yer gobblers,'" the farmer said. He left, and Mama soon realized that all her fat gobblers and big hens had been replaced by skinny birds. "'Our turkey check'll be pretty slim this year,'" she predicted.

"All our checks were pretty slim that winter," Grace reported. Mama was paid less for her eggs. The price of food went up. The McCances started cutting corners anywhere they could. "Mama let out the hems and waistbands on last year's dresses for us to wear to school, and patched the patches on our everyday clothes. The only new dresses we had were the ones she made from the cloth that came out of the Missouri barrels."

Poppie kept saying things would get better. In spite of a dry winter, he planted spring seed, certain the rains would come. They did not. "Almost no rains fell that terrible year," Grace said, "and what little there was came on winds so hard that it hadn't time to soak into the baked ground, but ran instead down the slopes into the cracked lagoons, where it was licked up in a day or two by the blazing sun and the hot, never-ending wind."

Grace began herding cattle as soon as school was out. She had turned twelve that spring of 1894, and Uncle John said if she would herd his cattle along with hers, he would give her a little red heifer in payment. The calf had been born on a freezing January night, and most of her tail had frozen off, but Grace did not care. "She was an odd-looking little beast, I know, but to me she was beautiful. I named her Bess and loved her all her life." Her hope was that, if Bess had a calf in a couple of years, she could sell it and buy herself a saddle.

"All that hot, dry summer I gave Bess special care. I hunted out the greenest spots in the dried-up pastures for her, and brushed her pretty coat to keep the burrs out of it. She hadn't enough tail left to switch flies off herself, so I helped her out by swinging a fly-chaser of weeds over her back and legs for hours at a time."

The cows were already thin from sparse winter rations. With almost no grass in the pastures, all of them grew thinner and thinner. The pigs had no corn for feed. Poppie put Stella and Dovey to work herding the cows and had Grace and Florry take the pigs to the wheat field every day to root out what little nourishment they could get from the hard, faded plants.

"Each day seemed hotter than the one before," Grace recalled. "The sun came up blazing, sailed all day through a glittering, brassy sky, and set in a smothering blast of heat that lasted all through the night. The burning winds moaned endlessly across the prairie and there was seldom even a thunderhead to break the sameness of sun and heat." Then, in late July, there was a day that was the hottest yet. Because Mama was sick, Florry stayed with her, and Poppie helped Grace with the pigs. They watched as a big cloud began to gather in the northwest sky—the first they had seen in weeks. For a while, Poppie was hopeful it might bring a little rain. He had to run an errand in the afternoon, so Grace was alone with the pigs when the air became so still and thick that it was hard to breathe. The cloud grew more threatening. Grace wished Poppie were with her.

"I watched the cloud uneasily while I circled the restless pigs, keeping them together the best I could in case I had to start for the house in a hurry. Then, late in the afternoon, the cloud suddenly began to bloom across the sky, like a black shawl flung out by the wind, and I knew it was time to go."

For once, the pigs were cooperative and practically flew across the prairie toward home. Florry had corralled the cattle and came running to help Grace pen the pigs. Poppie was just returning and yelled at the top of his voice, "'Hurry, girls, get to the house! This looks bad.'"

They could barely hear him above the roar of the wind. "We were halfway to the house when a wind as hot as a red-hot stove whirled out of the cloud and almost knocked us off our feet." Poppie said they had to get to the cellar. Florry and Stella helped Mama and the little girls. While Poppie shut off the windmill, Grace tried to close the windows in the house. "Dust, leaves, and dry grass filled the air and the wind seemed to screech against the awful, greenish purple cloud; then the storm shut out the last bit of light and I couldn't see anything at all."

Grace knew she had to get to the cellar. She ran outside, but the storm pushed her back against the door, knocking the wind out of her. Gasping for breath, unable to see, she suddenly felt Poppie's hand grab hers and pull her to the cellar. "Behind us there was a rip and a bang as the entry tore loose from the house. Then the boiler lid, snatched from its nail beside the boiler, flew past my ear with a screaming whistle. All at once we stumbled against the cellar door, and Poppie pulled it open and pushed me down the steps."

Poppie pulled the door closed, and immediately it was quiet. Grace tried to adjust her eyes to the darkness. Her sisters were all frightened, and the little ones were crying, Grace remembered. "We huddled there in the dark, musty-smelling cellar for quite a while. The roar of the storm was faint down there, under the thick dirt roof, and we couldn't tell what was going on outside."

When Poppie finally raised the door and looked out, the storm was blowing over fast and it was getting light outside. Slowly the family emerged. The house had been spared any serious damage, but everything else was a mess. The big grain bin was ruined. The corncrib was a twisted heap. The storage shed was destroyed, and so was the chicken house. Mama's chickens lay everywhere, all dead.

The family walked around in a daze. So much was ruined. Somewhere Grace could hear a kitten crying. She and her sisters finally located the sound under a pile of broken boards. Poppie helped move

These settlers survey the destruction caused by a big storm, just as Grace and her family did at their farm.

them, and they found a tiny kitten—the only survivor of a week-old litter. As she stroked the trembling kitten, Grace watched her father. He was digging into the dirt with the end of a split board. "'See,' he said, 'dry dirt! That rain hardly dampened the ground. Unless we get more in a day or two, there'll be no show for a crop of any kind this year.'"

Hard Times

No rain came. The McCances cleaned up the damage from the storm. Poppie said they were lucky it had not been a tornado that had struck that July afternoon or they might not have a house. All home-steaders lived in fear of funnel clouds, which usually occurred on sticky, still summer afternoons. If a "twister" touched the ground, it could destroy everything in its path.

After the storm, the McCance fields might as well have been through a tornado. Harvesttime came and went. For the second year in a row, there was nothing to harvest.

Water in shallow lagoons dried up. The well was fed by an under-ground spring, so the McCances still had well water. They used it to water Mama's garden, which produced food for the family, but there was no way to irrigate the crops. Grace watched what was happening to her neighbors: "Some families, certain that nothing but starvation was ahead, sold for what little they could get and pulled out." Many stayed because they could not afford to leave.

"Mama patched and 'made over' and patched some more, trying to get us girls ready for school in October," Grace said. "For by then, like almost everyone else in the community, we were down to our bottom dollar and supplies were running low. Poppie would have gladly 'hired out,' but no one had anything for a hired man to do, or money to pay him with if they had."

People in the East sent flour, coal, food, and clothing to each school district to be divided among the needy. With that help, people got by. Grandpa Blaine sent the McCances an extra barrel of molasses, which Poppie shared with neighbors. He did not have the heart to turn anybody away, so he ended up handing out most of the family's barrel of molasses as well.

Grace had trouble seeing the bright side of things that fall. Not only was there the drought but people were also getting sick or being hurt in accidents. A neighbor, Johnny Belstrom, died unexpectedly a moment after saying in a surprised voice, "'I don't feel good.'" Mama let Grace and Florry go with Poppie to the funeral.

Seeing Johnny's body in his coffin made Grace think about death. "I thought about Johnny, wondering what had become of all his memories and thoughts, right up to the noontime when he died. Where were his thoughts now, and all the things he had known? Did they just stop when his mind stopped, or did they go on somewhere? I knew souls went to heaven, but where did thoughts go, or did they just come to an end and be wasted?"

She missed the funeral for the minister's daughter who died during a brief outbreak of scarlet fever, because Poppie and Mama kept the girls home while there was fever around. A short time later a four-year-old they knew died of pneumonia. She was buried in a homemade coffin and mourned by her nine brothers and sisters.

Mama worried constantly about her six daughters. Danger lurked in many places for children. When times were hard, hungry children were not strong enough to resist common illnesses like the flu. Cholera, typhoid, diphtheria, scarlet fever, or smallpox could claim every child in a family.

There were other dangers. Settlers' children sometimes fell off wagons and were run over. They hunted and had accidents with guns. They fell into wells, were bitten by poisonous snakes, and were burned in campfires and fireplaces. They were caught in farm machinery. They fell off horses and were gored by bulls. They drowned in farm ponds, were struck by lightning, and were burned by boiling water or their mother's irons. They were hit by trains when they played on the railroad tracks.

Sometimes they got lost. Mama always worried about the girls wandering off and being unable to find their way home. The frantic parents of two little boys who disappeared into tall prairie grass finally had to give up looking for them. Eleven days later the father happened to stumble upon the boys several miles from their sod house. They were so weak from hunger they could not move. The father got them home by carrying them on his back, one at a time. He would carry one a short distance, then put him down and go back for the other, never letting either one out of his sight. Both boys recovered completely. It was a rare family that never lost at least one child at birth or to accident or illness. The McCances were lucky.

Funerals for children were common, and they were always sad. Sometimes children were photographed in their coffins because their parents had no other photos to remember them by. Children were usually buried in plain pine coffins with their heads resting on small satin pillows. Sometimes they would be buried with a favorite toy. If a mother and baby both died in childbirth, they were buried with the baby in the mother's arms. Where the McCances lived, funerals were usually held at home. Neighbors brought flowers and food and would sit up with the family the night before the service. Before there were churches and cemeteries, bodies were usually buried on the homestead and the graves cared for by the family.

This family is visiting the grave of a child who has died.

Mama worked hard at keeping her family healthy. She kept various patent medicines on hand that she bought from peddlers or at stores in town. There were hundreds of different kinds of patent medicines, most of them worthless and some actually dangerous. But few people lived where there was a doctor, so they used them, along with various homemade medicines. Grandma had a variety of these. A favorite was cough syrup made of onions mashed in sugar. And when Grace and her sisters had whooping cough, Grandma advised Mama to mix equal parts of strained honey, olive oil, and whiskey to help soothe their throats.

When Grace suffered a serious dog bite, "Mama fussed over me and made my favorite desserts and I didn't have to help with the dishes or do anything else I did not want to. I couldn't remember when Mama had ever babied me before. I used to watch her fussing over the newest baby and ache for the affection she never had time to show us older ones. But my top place in the sun of her tenderness didn't last long. In spite of myself I was well again in two days."

The family's most frightening incident was Poppie's attack of appendicitis. He was very ill for several weeks, growing steadily worse, unable to eat, and in terrible pain. Doctors at the time did not know how to operate on such cases, and Poppie's doctor said nothing more could be done: "His words were a death sentence, and Poppie shut his eyes and accepted it."

The rest of the family could not. They took turns sitting by Poppie's bed, sponging his face with cold water. One night, Grace recalled, "I was alone with Poppie, trying to prepare myself to give him up. I didn't see how I could do it, how I could ever get along without him. . . . He had taught me so many things I needed to know. I thought of all the good times we had had, singing together, and of the times he had taken Florry and me to picnics and ball games. I even thought of the times he had been stern and cross to me, and now I could see the need, and be grateful for those times, too."

When morning came, Poppie was still alive, and he was alive the morning after that. Then he started to get better, and they knew he would survive. When the day came that he could get up and get dressed, "he was so thin he could wrap his shirt and pants twice around himself."

As soon as he could travel, Poppie went to town to pay a little something on his doctor's bill. "The doctor stared at Poppie as if he had seen a ghost, then he jumped up and clapped him on the back. 'I never expected to see you again,'" he said.

Illnesses could also be mental, especially during hard times like the drought. Once in a while, Poppie and Mama would hear rumors that a death reported in the paper as accidental was actually a suicide. They knew settlers who despaired or even became insane. Overworked, lonely women were the most likely to suffer deep depression. Winter was the most difficult time. Men were outside every day and went to town for supplies whenever the weather allowed, so they were around people more than their wives. Women were often confined to the dark, cramped space of a soddy.

Some said the relentless, mournful wind could drive women mad, knocking on the doors and rattling the windows and keeping everything dusty all the time. There was a special term, *prairie women,* to describe the wives and mothers brought into mental asylums for depression.

Neither Poppie nor Mama were going to give in to despair. But in September, when Grace helped Poppie cut the last of the withered cornstalks and haul them to the stable, "he looked at the measly stack of dusty fodder a long time. Finally he said, 'We'll have to sell the cattle, Grace.' It must have cost him a lot to say that. I was stunned.

"'All of them?' I asked. 'Even Bess?'

"'Even Bess. There's no feed, and they'll starve if we try to keep them over the winter.'"

To save Bess, Grace took a heavy corn knife and went over the land, cutting every stray wisp of corn, grass, or weed she could find. "But it was no use. In all that burned valley there wasn't enough extra feed to keep one little bob-tailed heifer through the winter."

Several days later Poppie took the cattle to town. Grace could hardly stand it. Why was life so difficult? She moped around all day, but when Poppie returned that evening, all the cows were with him. Grace tried not to show how happy she was to have Bess back, because her father was "more beaten and discouraged than I had ever seen him.

'Maggie, I don't know what we're going to do this winter,' he told Mama. 'I couldn't sell the cattle. I couldn't even *give* 'em away. Everybody else is trying to sell, too, and nobody has any feed or any money. There's hardly a dollar in the whole country.'"

Grace was just glad that Bess had been spared.

ELEVEN

Grace Grows Up

As the drought continued, the cattle grew weaker. One day Poppie stopped by their old homestead and saw the dried-up corn stalks standing in the fields. The owner had no livestock, so Poppie was able to trade supplies for them. They were poor feed, but they kept the cows alive, including Bess.

The prairie was still like a furnace in the fall of 1894. Times were at their very worst when the seventh McCance baby was born. As usual, the girls had not known a baby was expected. One afternoon Poppie met them at the door when they came home from school and told them they had a baby *brother*. The first son born in the family of six daughters cheered everybody. Poppie and Mama named him Charles Roy—Roy for short.

Gradually the drought disappeared. By the spring of 1895, when Grace turned thirteen, "Good crops grew again and new grass covered and healed the scars on the prairie. Homesteaders, their faith in Nebraska restored once more, got busy with new plans."

Mama told Grace and Florry they were too old to go barefoot any longer. That was fine with Florry, who always acted like a lady. But even though Grace wanted to act grown up, she still longed "to feel warm cow trail dust and cool green grass" on her bare feet.

However, she thought she should try to act more like Florry if she wanted a special beau. She had her chance on Valentine's Day that following winter when Aunt Hester gave a party at Grandma's for all the young people in the valley. Mama made new red plaid dresses for Florry, Grace, and Stella, and Poppie said they could walk across the field to Grandma's house by themselves—their first time to go anywhere at night without an adult along. Florry was sixteen, Grace fourteen, and Stella twelve. Aunt Hester had decorated the house with red hearts and ribbon streamers and baked little heart-shaped pies. Everybody played games and sang.

Grace acted very ladylike, and "Oss Brownfield chose me for his partner for all the games. Oss was fifteen and good-looking, and I felt so grown up that night that I didn't believe I'd mind not going barefoot when summer came again." She still daydreamed about her cowboy, "but Montgomery Ward didn't list cowboys and I didn't know how I was going to get one."

Oss Brownfield wanted to take her to several parties, but Poppie would not allow that because she was not yet sixteen. Even when she turned sixteen the spring of 1898, Poppie still proved difficult on the subject of boys. Grace envied Florry, who liked John Houk, a neighbor boy whom Poppie approved of. Florry was allowed to go on Sunday buggy rides with him.

John and a friend asked Grace and Florry to go to Buffalo Bill Cody's Wild West Show. It would be held September 3 in North Platte, forty miles away. Poppie agreed they could go, if it was okay with Mama. "But Mama wouldn't say, one way or the other. The best we could get from her was an uncertain 'wait and see.' Even on the morning of September 2, she still said we'd have to 'wait and see.'"

That afternoon Grace and Florry were amazed to learn that Mama was going into labor. As old as they were, they had not known a baby

Grace (seated) was sixteen and Florry was eighteen when they posed for this formal picture in 1898.

was expected. The doctor came, and Grace zoomed across the fields to fetch Grandma. By nightfall, the family welcomed a new baby girl. They named her Esther, but Mama called her Sweetheart, soon shortened to Heart.

Florry and Stella started school in the fall, but sixteen-year-old Grace worked in the fields, helping Poppie bring in the corn crop. They finished on a cold day in late November, and Poppie told Grace she could start school the next day. She resisted, arguing that she would be one of the oldest students, and too far behind. Poppie listened and then said he did not want her to drop out of school, as he had. She started school the next day.

Grace's teacher was kind to her. She understood that some children could go to school only when they were not needed at home. Many

Some men, like the one shown here with his students in front of their school, made teaching their career, but most teachers were young girls.

teachers were the daughters of homesteaders, so they knew how hard children worked to help their families. The teachers worked hard, too, and often brought textbooks from their meager wages. Teachers were paid so little that they usually boarded with students' families.

Grace's teacher worked especially hard, for many of the children in the school spoke Swedish and were just starting to learn English. In addition to preparing lessons, the teacher took care of the school building. A one-room sod building like Grace's school was difficult to keep clean. The teacher also came early each day to build a fire so the room was warm when the students got there. After they left, she swept and dusted.

With her teacher's help, Grace soon caught up in her studies. She found that she loved poetry and spelling. Then, in December, just a month after Grace had started back to school, a middle-aged bachelor named Old Bill Sherman stopped by the house at dinnertime. Old Bill was well educated and fond of quoting Shakespeare. Grace thought of him as "a man of means—and a bum by choice" because he wore castoff clothing and rarely bathed.

While he ate their dinner, Old Bill said that he knew Poppie was looking for more pastureland for his cattle and that he had a good place along the Birdwood Creek, sixty-five miles away, that he would like to rent out. He described the lush grasses for cattle and the winding creek with big trees on the bank near the house. A school was close by.

Poppie thought it sounded like just what he was looking for. He could increase his cattle herd, and Mama would be away from the dust that made her cough persistently. But when Mama asked about the house, Old Bill admitted it had only four rooms. Poppie said that was too small for his family, so Old Bill offered to add on a big room. Before he left that evening, the deal was closed.

Grace was seventeen when the family moved to the Birdwood. The house was small, dark, dirty, and infested with bedbugs. Once again Mama had no front parlor. She said it would be better once Old Bill added on the new room. She was coughing much less, and she was happy living beside a creek with trees and hills around her.

Grace liked having fresh water at hand, and she loved the shade of the big trees, but she felt lonely. Florry, who had always been her best friend, was busy making plans for her wedding to John Houk. Then Stella began spending all her time with a new beau.

One blazing hot day in July when Grace was alone in the house, "a slim gray-eyed young man with black hair and mustache stood at the door, his wide-brimmed cowboy hat in his hand." His name was Bert

Because the work was dirty and exhausting, most cowboys were young men who rarely stayed with it more than a few years.

Snyder. Grace and Bert chatted briefly. Then "the cowboy put his hat back on his head, swung up on his tall gray horse, and rode on down the creek. I watched him go, the first cowboy I had ever seen, and so polite and friendly, too. He rode better than anyone I had ever observed on a horse, so easy and graceful."

Florry was married in October of 1899. Mama made her wedding dress, and Grace helped prepare the wedding dinner. Old Bill had added a new room to the little house, and that was where the ceremony was held. After the wedding, Florry and John moved back near the old homestead. Grace wondered how she would ever get along without her sister.

Rather than attend a new school, Grace spent the winter with Uncle John and his family and went to her old school. For a while, she "kept company" with a young man interested in her, but in the spring she returned to the Birdwood, feeling at loose ends.

One evening she was in the barn milking when Old Bill Sherman came and started chatting with her. Then he said, "'Well, Grace, I been a-thinkin' if we wuz t' get married. What do ye' say t' that, huh?'"

Shocked, Grace almost knocked her stool over: "I was so mad I couldn't say anything at first, then I remembered that he was our landlord—so all I said was that I wasn't ever going to get married."

Old Bill's proposal forced Grace to make a decision: "Most of the girls I knew, unless they married early, went into other people's kitchens as hired girls, or became clerks or schoolteachers." Only teaching interested her. When she mentioned this to Poppie, he said he would help her attend the teachers' institute in North Platte the following summer. They went to the bank and he cosigned a loan for the thirty-five dollars she needed to pay for room, board, tuition, and classroom supplies.

Her summer was all planned when, in the spring of 1901, Mama gave birth to her ninth baby, Earl Blaine. Mama was so weak afterward that Florry, who had a way with babies, came to care for Earl. Grace loved having her sister there. She wanted to stay home and help, but Poppie insisted she go ahead with her plans. She reluctantly packed her bags and said good-bye to her family for the first time in her life.

Her summer in North Platte turned out to be wonderful. She lived with other girls her age and she enjoyed her studies. She worked hard. After passing all her examinations, she was asked by the director to take a teaching position in the sandhills—a vast, sparsely settled area of western and northern Nebraska. Grace did not want to be so far from home, but she accepted.

Before she left, she saw Bert Snyder one more time. She had ridden up the creek to pick chokecherries, and her horse had gotten away from her. She was trying to grab at the reins, her skirt hitched up to keep it from getting wet, when he came around the bend on his gray horse. Grace never forgot what happened next. "I yanked my skirt down over my knees and stood there, feeling like my bare feet were all over the ground. The cowboy caught my horse and led her back to me. 'Looks like you're having a little trouble.' He grinned as he handed me the reins, then lifted his hat and rode on up the creek. As soon as he was out of sight, I climbed on old Daisy, popped her a good one with the ends of the reins, and headed back to the cherry patch. It seemed that I just hadn't been born to charm cowboys."

Stella was married that October, just before Grace left for the sandhills. In spite of her poor schooling as a child, Grace was now better educated than most homesteaders' daughters. She was twenty years old and had a determined will that helped her get through the long months in the sandhills. She lived with a ranch family and taught their two sons—her only pupils. The ranch was very isolated, and there was no one her age nearby. When she was not teaching, she quilted.

When the school year ended, she accepted a teaching position near her family, moved back to the Birdwood, and worked at making herself a good teacher. "I was twenty-one now, and it didn't look like I was ever going to be a cowboy's bride. So, if I was going to have to make teaching my life's work, I meant to make the most of it."

Then a girlfriend invited her to a fish fry, and Bert Snyder was there. They fried fish together and ate together. When everyone went berry picking, Bert stayed with Grace. "When we were out of earshot of the others, he told me he'd like to bring an extra saddle horse, come Sunday, and take me riding. I said I'd be glad to go, and that he'd better come early enough to eat dinner with us."

Grace knew she was in love. That Sunday Bert came on the tall gray. Just as in Grace's daydreams, back when she was herding cattle, he was leading a saddled horse for her. The two of them rode down the creek and stopped at a shady place. Grace could see that he was "studying something over in his mind." They sat on the grass and talked, and then he asked her to marry him. Absolutely sure of herself, Grace answered, "Yes." He looked surprised and then he let out a long breath. "'Good!' he said. 'I sure was afraid I'd have to put up a big talk before you'd say that.'"

TWELVE

The Quilt Lady of Nebraska

Grace married her cowboy in October 1903 at his parents' home in Maxwell, Nebraska. After the wedding, they left for the ranch Bert now had in the sandhills, stopping just before sunset to camp for the night. "We sat on the stubbly meadow grass beside the wagon and ate our wedding supper, while the warm autumn night settled down around us," Grace remembered. They slept under the stars, and the next morning they stopped in North Platte to have their wedding picture taken. Then they worked their way north and west over the grass-covered sandhills.

As they rode, Grace learned more about her new husband. Bert was thirty-one—ten years older than she. He had been a cowboy since he was fifteen, had ridden on many cattle drives, and had turned down a chance to join Buffalo Bill Cody's Wild West Show. He had a gift for storytelling and loved to read. Like other men in the sandhills, he always wore a Stetson hat, cowboy boots, and jeans.

Late in the afternoon, when Grace first saw Bert's ranch, she immediately felt she belonged there. Her new home was a big sod house with a sturdy tin roof. Using the skills she had learned from Mama, she soon had it feeling cozy and cheerful. She decorated the house with her beautiful quilts, and she filled the sunny windowsills with pots of flowers she coaxed into blooming.

Grace and Bert Snyder's wedding portrait

From the very beginning, Grace loved being a ranch wife and she loved the sandhills, even though the area was sparsely settled and the poor roads made it difficult to travel to see her family. She felt especially isolated from them when her first baby, a girl, was stillborn, and none of them could be with her. A year later Nellie Irene was born, and when she was a few months old, Grace took her to meet Mama and Poppie. They had just moved into a new house built of wood. It had a proper front parlor for Mama and elegant new furniture. Grace recalled, "I looked at Mama, so frail and wispy, standing there in the middle of her parlor, and suddenly I understood what that room meant to her. It was her symbol of prosperity; it meant that she had won out over all the hard years when she'd had to have a bed in her front room."

When Poppie was in his late sixties, he was hit and killed by a swerving car. Mama lived several years longer. Shortly before her death, when Grace went to see her, she talked about her twenty grandchildren and about Poppie and their homestead days. By then, Mama had lost not only Poppie but also Florry. The fall of 1908, Grace had spent several days with Florry, who at last was expecting a child. The next spring, just after giving birth to a healthy daughter, Florry died. For the rest of her life, Grace would miss the sister who had been her best friend.

Florry's death made Grace treasure all the more her life with Bert and their children. Their son, Miles William, was born in 1906. Then came two more daughters. Billie Lee was born in 1913. She was followed a year later by Bertie, whose full name was Flora Alberta: Flora for Florry, and Alberta for Bert, whose real name was Albert.

Grace raised her children with great care. They were expected to help on the ranch. All were expert riders and rode horseback to their one-room schoolhouse. If school closed for lack of students, and it

Nellie, Bertie, and Billie

often did, Grace taught them at home, for she did not want them to have gaps in their education, as she did.

Life in the sandhills was never dull. Grace was the area's postmaster for a while, running the post office from a room off the kitchen. Through the years, the family experienced runaway horses, hailstorms that pounded everything flat, dust storms, prairie fires, blizzards, and even a neighborhood murder that had Bert riding posse looking for the killer. That was the only time Grace regretted having no locks on the doors.

Grace lived through a time of great change. Bert bought one of the first automobiles in the sandhills in 1913. It often broke down on the terrible roads, but to Grace, who had always traveled on horseback or by wagon, the car was a wonder. In 1917 they got their first telephone, and in the mid-1920s they added electricity and indoor plumbing. By then, they had already been living for twenty years in a ranch house built of wood, with porches running the full length of the front and back. Grace never lived in a sod house again.

In spite of electricity and indoor plumbing, day-to-day work on the ranch was physically demanding and never finished. Grace cared for the children, managed the house, helped with the ranch chores, tended chickens, and raised vegetables and flowers in her garden. She made all her daughters' clothes, canned vegetables, and cured meats. If a neighbor needed any kind of assistance, she helped. Like Mama and Grandma McCance before her, she had no time on her hands.

Yet Grace still found time to create exquisite quilts. On the prairie, quilting was a way women could express their artistry and creativity, while making bedding for everyday use. During long winter evenings on the ranch, when the children did homework and Bert read, Grace

Grace used 5,400 yards of thread in her famous Flower Basket Petit Point quilt.

quilted. No one could hand stitch a more perfect circle than she could. She often included pieces of cloth from her children's favorite clothing in her beautiful designs. Years later they could look at a quilt and recall an outfit they had once worn.

During World War II, when gas and tire rationing made it difficult to go anywhere, Grace created the group of "show" quilts that brought her fame. Her masterpiece, the Flower Basket Petit Point, had 87,789 pieces and gave her the reputation of being the "Quilt Lady of Nebraska." It took her sixteen months and 5,400 yards of thread to make it, and it was a sensation at quilt exhibits.

Grace and Bert's children all married happily and pursued many interests. Nellie Snyder Yost was a writer. Miles took over the ranch. Billie Snyder Thornburg was a dancer and dance teacher. Bertie Snyder Elfeldt was a busy ranch wife with a special interest in horses.

Bert suffered a stroke in 1956, when he was eighty-four. Grace was holding his hand when he died. "I think it was a real love match with the two of them," Billie said. "They didn't have much of a courtship, but Dad had an idea about her. He watched her for a while before he rode up on that horse. As for Mother, once she saw her gray-eyed cowboy, that was it for her."

Grace lived for nearly thirty more years. She died in her sleep a few months after her one hundredth birthday, in 1982. "Mother was a true pioneer," Bertie said. "She had that special spirit. I'll never forget one time she came to visit me at my ranch. She was getting on in years, and I suggested we go into town to visit a dress shop she liked. I thought maybe we would have some lunch and just make an easy day of it. But she said if it was all the same to me, she'd rather go rattlesnake hunting.

"So we did, and we killed quite a few that day."

When pioneer homesteaders first came to the prairie, lots of people thought they were foolish to try to cultivate that land. But they broke the tough sod, nurtured crops and cattle, and turned the Midwest into a region of farms and ranches. Working alongside them were their children.

Most pioneer children did not know how hard their lives were. They just did what had to be done. One pioneer child said, "No matter what happened, we always planned on next year being a good year and never quite gave up, for along with all the hard work and worry we had lots of fun and good times."

That is how it was for Grace. When she reflected on all that had happened to her over the years, she said, "I couldn't have asked for a more wonderful life."

*Grace mounted this horse on her
ninetieth birthday.*

GRACE McCANCE SNYDER
1882-1982
Nebraska pioneer
loving daughter, wife, mother, and grandmother
inspired quiltmaker

Further Reading

YOUNG READERS

Chu, Daniel, and Bill Shaw. *Going Home to Nicodemus: The Story of an African American Frontier Town and the Pioneers Who Settled It.* Morristown, NJ: Julian Messner, 1994.

Duncan, Dayton. *The West: An Illustrated History for Children.* Boston: Little, Brown, 1996.

Freedman, Russell. *Children of the Wild West.* New York: Clarion, 1983.

Greenwood, Barbara. *A Pioneer Sampler.* New York: Ticknor & Fields, 1995.

Murphy, Jim. *Across America on an Emigrant Train.* New York: Clarion, 1993.

Wilder, Laura Ingalls. The Little House Books. New York: HarperCollins.

OLDER READERS AND ADULTS

Cather, Willa. *My Ántonia.* Boston: Houghton Mifflin, 1918.

Dale, Edward Everett. *Frontier Ways.* Austin: University of Texas Press, 1989.

Riley, Glenda. *The Female Frontier.* Lawrence: University Press of Kansas, 1988.

Snyder, Grace, as told to Nellie Snyder Yost. *No Time on My Hands.* Lincoln: University of Nebraska Press, 1986.

Stratton, Joanna L. *Pioneer Women.* New York: Simon & Schuster, 1981.

West, Elliot. *The Way West.* Albuquerque: University of New Mexico Press, 1995.

Acknowledgments

At the start of this project, I met with members of Grace's family in the North Platte, Nebraska, home of her great-granddaughter, Jo Morphew. Over coffee and homemade cinnamon rolls, they recalled memories of Grace that enrich this book. I am especially grateful to Jo, and to her father, Thomas Yost, for their assistance. A very special thanks goes to Grace's daughters, Billie Snyder Thornburg and Bertie Snyder Elfeldt, for sharing their loving remembrances of their mother. Billie not only contributed many of the photos in this book, but she also showed me several of Grace's beautiful quilts, helping me to understand the effort and skill that went into each stitch.

My thanks to Regina Ryan, to Judy Levin, and to the staff at William Morrow for their support and assistance in ways large and small; and to Barbara Bartocci, Deborah Shouse, and Mildred's for all those invaluable Friday mornings. As always, I couldn't do this without my husband, Jay Wiedenkeller, who makes life fun.

I wish I could thank Nellie Snyder Yost, now deceased, for the wonderful memoir she wrote for her mother; and Dorothy Creigh, also deceased, for her book, *Nebraska* (New York: W. W. Norton, 1977), which helped me see my native state with fresh eyes.

Photo Credits

The author is grateful to the following for the use of their photos: the family of Grace McCance Snyder—pp. 3, 5, 56–57, 75, 83, 85, 86, 88; the Kansas State Historical Society—pp. 8, 15, 19, 21, 27, 30, 36, 38, 41, 49, 50, 55, 76, 78; the Nebraska State Historical Society—pp. 10, 13, 23, 32, 46, 65, 69.

Index